Laying Out Tomorrow's Outfit

poems by

Andy Feathers

Finishing Line Press
Georgetown, Kentucky

Laying Out Tomorrow's Outfit

Copyright © 2016 by Andy Feathers
ISBN 978-1-944251-47-5 First Edition
All rights reserved under International and Pan-American Copyright Conventions. No part of this book may be reproduced in any manner whatsoever without written permission from the publisher, except in the case of brief quotations embodied in critical articles and reviews.

ACKNOWLEDGMENTS

Some of these poems have appeared, been awarded by, or are forthcoming in the journals listed below:

Carbon Culture Review: "Unreachable, Lost in Canoe Creek" and "Letters from a Lover in the Land Before Texting"
Festival Writer: "My America," "NEWS!," and "Texts with Friends Part I, To: Carmen";
Insistent Light Poetry Contest: "Unreachable, Lost in Canoe Creek"
The Poetry Explosion Newsletter: "Remembering When I Lost My Virginity"
Turbulence Magazine: "Laying Out Tomorrow's Outfit"
After Happy Hour Review: "This Way This Fast"

Editor: Christen Kincaid

Cover Art: Sadie Shoaf

Author Photo: Katie Krulock

Cover Design: Elizabeth Maines

Printed in the USA on acid-free paper.
Order online: www.finishinglinepress.com
   also available on amazon.com

Author inquiries and mail orders:
Finishing Line Press
P. O. Box 1626
Georgetown, Kentucky 40324
U. S. A.

Table of Contents

Unreachable, Lost in Canoe Creek 1

i want 2

Remembering When I Lost My Virginity 5

Kenny Chesney Tailgate in Gold Lot 1A 6

She's Another 9

I Love You 11

Texts with Friends Part I, To: Carmen 12

Goals 13

My America 14

This Way This Fast 15

Like When I was a Kid 16

Laying Out Tomorrow's Outfit 17

My Dog Died This Afternoon 18

Entrepreneurs 20

Letters from a Lover in the Land Before Texting 22

This Way This Fast Part II 23

Not Ready Yet 25

Texts with Friends Part XI, To: Adrienne 26

NEWS! 27

In January, Crossing the Mississippi 28

When I'm Depressed I Say Things Like 29

Eat 'n Park Poem 31

Texts with Friends Part XV, To: Sadie 32

To everyone I love in reality and sometimes digitally, and my old dogs Rudy and Spencer. Rudy for his dedication, and Spencer, for that one look that couldn't be mistaken as empty.

Unreachable, Lost in Canoe Creek

over the lip of a cliff
a dogwood juts out
like a two-finger peace sign
rooted in the dirt, with space
just open enough to cradle
the width of my shoulders
& closed on an angle flush
with my legs

lying out over the lake
watching osprey make
their rounds, polarized eyes
locked on to ripe pickerel
too meaty to fly away with
or forget about

the hills clear their collective
throat & a warm wind plays
on the brown cuffs of the water,
a newt buries himself in the mud
at the motion &

my phone vibrates, to tell me
about an acquaintance's
great new recipe
for low-fat cupcakes

i want

i want this to be read on a piece of paper,
& talked about at a coffee shop
by people who aren't quite sure
what they're reading or why they like it,

i want at least one of them to be 26
or 24, wanting the same things i want,
our generation to ship its ascent overnight,
past our stockpile of over-disclosed trifles,
poorly conceptualized short film-making & bass,

i want to be impossible to market to,
i want historians to research for millennia
trying to sort & pin-down our plot points,

i want to keep deleting this capital "i"
& the first letter of every new line
until spell-check-auto-correct lets me keep them
lowercase, leave my seatbelt unfastened,
& swim in the windshield if i want to,

i don't want to be a virtual being, lost
in the air when my greatest nephew
caveman, ten thousand years from now
can no longer access it, when man is
no longer master of the plastic squares

i want to be dug up somewhere, between
wood or cardboard covers, & examined,
laughed at, lying there bloodless
& bleeding all over the hands of whoever
dug me up,

i want to break up with you in a letter,
so we're both over each other by the time
our responses arrive,

& i want you to flash me your breasts now,
when i can do something with them,
instead of myself & a thousand
little pixels you sent, doing their best
& failing miserably,

i want to make enough money,
so i don't have to feel bad
about not giving a shit whether or not
i make enough money, & i want a woman
who cares even less. i want to find her,

i want to make loin-cloths fashionable again,
& age an option like leather seats & sun-roofs,
i want to perpetually relive the best concerts
of my first, second, & third favorite bands,

to live forever as a Rorschach ink stain
that never gets the same response twice
& becomes a symbol for individuality
& eventually put on the front of millions
of white v-neck t-shirts, everyone wears,

the same tattoo thousands of people
who don't know each other all have,
i want to be that classic symbol of irony,

i want to write a meta-poem, i want
this poem to be that meta-poem, & i want
it to be over with now,
since it's slowing down & losing ground,

i want to move on to something pithier,
shorter—at least—at least shorter,

more marketable, a self-published blog,
so it might be stumbled upon accidentally
during a google search, read, & lost
into someone's subconscious,
i want to be a hypocrite,

& then when someone is drawn in to hypocrisy,
loin-cloths, & living forever,
i want them to try & find out why,
& i want to be found.

Remembering When I Lost My Virginity

After "I Can't Quit Her" by Blood, Sweat & Tears

The second you let your forearm, two years younger than mine,
cradling your energetic breasts, fall,
during that game of Pa-diddle in my parents car,
& they encompassed the full landscape of my rearview mirror,
i knew it was you who Al Kooper was talking about,
who had made a man out of him,
& was soon to proselytize me, two romantic nights later
after we shared a strawberry Phillies blunt
leaning against the bumper of my Ford Taurus SE—X.
Our cotton mouths met in remorseless piano solos,
fading into repeating vocal refrains,
which i will not repeat,
before we struggled to the back,
unseen in our nakedness behind the draped windows,
with fog from our breath, & smoke
from the chilled leather hissing on our salivating,
determined skin, as it met the Thanksgiving air.
It was a steady bass line then, a cool tambourine shake
like sprinkling a full container of parmesan cheese,
right before the good part,
& i licked awe, everywhere i thought i was supposed to
until the backwards guitar solo, when we both had to pee,
running out into the park behind red & yellow jungle gyms,
& swiftly back again, me on my back, & inside,
you, surrounding me, leaning for the right angle
like a high-tech protractor
as saxophones & trumpets tip-toed in & blew,
too early, repeating until it was done & gone,
& we stared at each other—blushing,
because the song faded
after a few catchy minutes,
but will not
get out
of our heads.

Kenny Chesney Tailgate in Gold Lot 1A

obviously it was a day-long,
6:30 a.m. at the latest, 5:00
just to be safe, 250 people,
with 20 cases, 20 handles,
2 kegs of Genny, 20 hot dogs,
2 half gallons of Heinz,
& an 8 pack of buns.

Keith couldn't find a ladder
tall enough to reach the top
of the eight foot octo-beer-bong
yet wide enough at the base
to fit inside the kiddy pool
& not wobble in the 500 pounds
of sand we poured over
the parking lot to create
the artificial beach we needed
in front of the tiki-bar

so Kathleen held the bong
steady while Pheifer stood
on an empty cooler to pour
in the beer for the eight
foaming chuggers below,
waiting for sustenance.

Zawilla told anyone who asked
that the bathroom was anywhere
on the other side of the cars,
where the sidewalk ran, it didn't
matter, as long as dumps were only
taken in the porta-johns, unless—
he pointed out—you saddled-up
next to Cenzo's driver's side door,
then it was too funny to stop you.

All the guys with muscles
or the idea of muscles
had their shirts off, so Paul moved
to join them, but Maddie said no,
if he took his shirt off,
then she would take hers off, too;
he reminded her that they weren't
dating anymore—he could do
whatever he wanted—

& i wondered if Maddie
remembered or would be
embarrassed if i reminded her
that Paul wasn't even the last
guy she dated, that i was—
called things quits only
two weeks ago & my shirt
was off, yet she was giving him
a hard time, & not me,
as if she was so drunk
her memory was even drunk,

like Rachel McAdams
in The Vow, that other Nicholas
Sparks book turned movie Maddie
raved about as we left the theatre,
where the heroine relives her life
over again out of amnesia,
back to the guy whose faults
were least fresh in her mind,
until fate's graces inevitably
end the scenario the same way,

the heroine with a human sculpture,
& Maddie on yet another search
for someone she can pause,
fast forward, and rewind.

we pre-gamed like this
until the concert was about
to start, & at that point,
stopped preparing & got down
to the business side of drinking

i went into the stadium to work
as a vendor, hawkin' brews
to fans for a shot at a big payday,
eight bucks a pop & a callous scowl
at the sobering price of revelry
while everyone else left
to hit the casino for the same

She's Another

my 17 year old sister is in love with her 18 year old boyfriend
of eight months.

we all sit in the living room of his parents beach house,
behind vacation's music,
& i watch from the couch as my parents play spades
with the two of them at the dining room table
like a family after a meal that included steamed broccoli,

i wonder what emotional jenga tower is teetering in her head,
the holes & shoddy appliqués she rigged over it last week
when he told her that he cheated on her
because she wasn't putting out,

during his third week of summer session at Pitt,
his pre-freshman semester,
how drunk & confused, but it's been so long since his last time
& he respects her decision to be abstinent but, you know. so like.
but still…

how sorry he was, how upset that this is all so poorly timed,
but he had to tell her before vacation, the guilt was just so—

oh, the guilt—& it would be up to her, whether he still comes
or not, whether she forgives him because he knows he fucked up,
& she cried,

doesn't know what to say each time my dad laughs at his college
story hijinks,
& my mom alludes to their future in old-fashioned blindness,

i watch her squinting, anticipating each new move, befuddled
by the closing gaps
as they roll together in the waves & he holds her up by the butt
over his head, lifts & then tosses her
into the breakers, she looks at me & knows what i'd say,
that i hope she's getting all the blocks together, that she's another
smart as any of us, that she's another knows what she's doing,
that she's another doing it anyway.

I Love You

When she said it
i said it back
& then started thinking
what this new verbalization
of our relationship means,
the actions that we'll both replace
with the words

Texts with Friends Part I
To: Carmen, 11:18 a.m., Wednesday, 4/9/14

Miss you out there in Utah, man.
I gotta tell ya, it's pretty weird.
It's the best weather we've had
yet this year in the Burgh. I'm
at work now, dickin' around,
singin' some My Morning Jacket.
You Wanna Freak Out?
Concert season is looming.
I'm gonna go get a case
of Lionshead, if you wanna
get in on it, I'll meetcha
dahn Stage AE in 30 minutes

Goals

Tomorrow i'll be doing what i want.
what i want, Tomorrow, i'll be doing.
i'll be doing what i want, Tomorrow.
Tomorrow, what i want, i'll be doing.
i'll be doing, Tomorrow, what i want.
what i want, i'll be doing Tomorrow.
Tomorrow, i want what i'll be doing.
i want what i'll be doing Tomorrow.
i want Tomorrow, doing what i'll be.
doing what i want,   i'll be Tomorrow.

My America

my light blue t-shirt,
soft like winter flannel bedding,
with navy blue block letters
reads *Siesta Key*,
& when people ask me
how i like it i say, *mmm...
it's so soft,*
& when they say *no*
they meant *Siesta Key*
i say *oh...
who the hell knows?
i've never been there.
i got this at a Goodwill
in Virginia Beach.*
they Laugh, & it makes me
want to find *Siesta Key*
on a map because,
like a lot of other things,
i'm not sure if it really exists
or is just written on something
that gets thinner after every wash

This Way This Fast

we're lying together in bed,
& you have fallen asleep on me
again, trying to finish the ending
of The 400 Blows, with half of your merlot
left, i empty my paper cup into myself
& start onto yours—

i hope tomorrow morning,
when you apologize for dozing off,
& shorting out on all the fun,
that you'll remember it was your idea
to drink & watch a movie
instead of get more work done
on the painting series you need to have
ready for your show in two weeks,

& when your anxiety kicks in,
& we begin its traditional remedy,
cleaning up all the clutter around the apartment,
wondering how it gets this way this fast,
i am going to kiss the left side of your mouth
with the right side of mine, like i'm doing now,
making sure not to let my cold sore, lazy
& contagious, touch your lips & transmit
to you, in this dark room

aside from the screen of the laptop & rotations
of green, pink & blue from the neon sign
across the street, the Chinese place
outside the window, occasionally lighting up
your yoga books on the floor,
everything breathing slowly with you,
i hold mine in a moment longer
to fall in line.

Like When I Was a Kid

there was a fire
on my street today
so i walked over
as close as i could get
to the scene
so the lights were shining
around me & i looked
red & yellow & stuff,

other people were watching
from their porches,
(but i don't have to tell you,
you know),

the firemen were brave,
& when i walked back
to my place, the people
who are smarter than me
asked why i felt the need
to be there,
& i lied & said
that i wanted to be around
in case i could help.
i lied & said
i thought
i could help
with saving people & stuff.

Laying Out Tomorrow's Outfit

If submission was not such an out of style vest
to put on in the morning after a bagel
& fat free whipped cinnamon spread,
    i would wear it more.   So it's brown and grey,
with coffee stains,   & washing machine fade,
    i *like* brown and grey clothing
the colors are so agreeable   *easy*,
fashion's   conversation   with an old friend
especially with jeans.   i could make it work,
i'll just put on a peppy   bright   cardigan,
red maybe? over top, & the Burberry scarf
i have from   Salvation Army around my neck
arranged so it hangs   down in front of my chest
& upper abdomen as extra   vest   blockage
A hat, too,   big furry ear flaps hanging down
off of a head piece that looks like scrap wool
from an old afghan,   just to draw gazes away
from the vest, ya know?   i'll wear my nice
boots,   with the oiled leather & white soul,
to add some   flash.   A jacket,   maybe,
would be good,   navy blue pea coat,   or black
like everyone in London wears,   & then
some lime green gloves   with Kermit the Frog's face
on each finger, a sort of, conversation piece,   yes?
Because i just want to wear my vest   unquestioned
without having to respond while i'm out
molding a life with the daylight,   standing
in lines & filling out forms for   _____ ,
with a lot of other   overdressed   fashionistas.

My Dog Died This Afternoon

my dog died this afternoon,
in my sister's arms with the rest of the family
around him, mom & dad, i imagine
in a little two-person semi-circle, crying
while i was at work, cussing
out the stupidity of cheap, impatient men

who will pay to have their pre-fabricated houses
delivered from Ohio, but won't spring
for the pre-painted siding—so now,
my friend, his dad, & me, have to figure
how we can most-efficiently paint
one thousand of these fire-retardant slats
some shit café latte color, & also try
to remember the name of the dirty magazine
Lloyd wants to buy in Dumb & Dumber
with the 'last of his dough,' (Rhode Island Slut).

As we run paint rollers therapeutically along
the textured side, his dad says
"that's one of the only movies i'd go see in the theatre,"
& i hope that when we're done here
i can just *do* that—movie in a theatre—

instead of going home to scroll the internet over dinner,
& see this picture of my dog's two vacant eyes,
posted socially & white with a fog & gloss
that only absence can therapeutically paint,
staring out towards something
i'll never be able to write about
or buy with the last of my dough
when my coat has thinned, my prostate so large
that my owners have to catheterize me, too,
in the stationary tub in their laundry room,

maybe, i hope, after seeming so stupid to them for so long,
i'll have his same omniscient stare, i'll sit outside—
chest filled with its last round of good air, dominating—
looking out at my yard, my rose bush, my slide, my fence,
my shed, my gazebo, & on its lot, with its shit colored siding,
my fucking pre-fabricated house,
painted as they cuss me out,
by cheap, impatient men.

Entrepreneurs

After a couple of bong rips each,
we stood in the kitchen drinking wine
& discussing incredible ideas for new businesses
using old businesses as platforms from which to jump.

Eli & Noska agreed that Eli was going to be Noska's talent agent
for modeling & acting, & in exchange, Noska would set Eli up
with a different girl every other day for the next 18 months
—   sevens or higher.

Sam got distracted & left with a bowl of cold chili
he took from a pot in the fridge & went into the living room,
& the rest of us realized that we also wanted bowls of chili,
with hot sauce, & Sam yelled in that it was okay with him.

As we ate, congregated around the table like it was a fire,
& we were a rag-tag band of cow-pokes, eating our beans
in ponchos & hide with work on our minds,
& our faces no more than six inches above our bowls,

Eli was on the innovative money. He developed a model
that would allow us to start our own late night cab service
& collaborate with locally run bars & restaurants to promise us
after hours transit customers in exchange for advertising—

but more than just signage, it would include the driver's scripted,
enthusiastic recommendation, improvised supportive testimony,
& a coupon for buy one, get one half off or whatever.
We would be the drivers, & pocket the money under the table.

It was only a matter of time, & we were high
on autonomy's brand-newness like standing up on water-skis
& riding the wakes, but more, like standing up on water skis
& riding the wakes behind twin dolphins, skimming across

the top of the breakers, close enough to shore for all the bikinis
to see.   We agreed that, eventually, we would sell the business
for $50-100 mil.,   & Noska—with a toddler's awe—
asked "Eli, what will it take to get all this started *right now?*"

& Sam, from the living room asked, "Eli! *Super-Mario?*"
& turning, Eli said, "Hell yeah *Super-Mario…*"

Letters from a Lover in the Land Before Texting

Looking through the paper
held up to the light,
adding to the suspense,
like pressing your eyes against a deep
sheet of ice to see a fossilized heart
frozen in a time—the image
of their hand, their words laid
out in loopy strokes on the page
inside, appearing as a friendly face
might before an embrace:
spotted behind some mob
on the opposite side of the bar;
clear enough only to say:
" Is *that*? ... It *is* ... "

This Way This Fast Part II

we're lying together in bed again,
the space heater set to six,
as high as it will go, and heating us
to the point where it is 18 degrees out,
and you're asleep naked on your stomach,
on top of the covers with your bare ass
angled towards me, and me, very much
the same only awake and on my back,
lay my left leg across yours, and wedge
my right toe between your calves
because i want to sweat with you a little.

Instead of wine, this time I'm finishing off
a Straub, and we're at the point in our
relationship now, where one of us is okay
with being asleep while the other is awake
without feeling like we're missing something,
that perpetual connectedness more mature.
but i am temporarily alone now, and taking
a break from reading Big Sur to marvel
at the heater's representation of man's ability
to overcome the elements, and it's relationship
to what Kerouac is saying about cabin life,

that simplicity is the only way to live,
and that he finds his in nature: seaside hiking
through the forest desert mountains,
wading through the creek river canyon
tundra to see the wild chimp horse natives,
learning meditations wine-addled around
a roadside campfire with the train-hoppers

he'd befriended while hitchhiking
to the mermaid-laden waterfalls on the way
back to his friend's pad in Greenwich village,
and all of life's other little simplicities
that sound like incredibly expensive
vacations to me now, ones i wonder how
he afforded, to find so much

simplicity in nature, so much simplicity
in that thing with the complexity
that still baffles scientists to shrugging,
those same scientists who developed this space
heater. But maybe that's what the thing is for,
making that move towards simplicity,
so i can look at you this way, cozy
and natural in Pittsburgh winter,

because surely Kerouac—after being published
en masse and credited for the birth
of a generation—is right, and we both know it,
deciding after several minutes of deliberation
that out of all the sets we have, we don't even
need pajamas tonight—naked in our one bedroom
above our 1800 sq. ft. studio, iphones on
Do Not Disturb, surrounded by vintage clothing,
our mini-pig at our feet and forearms decorated
with matching tattoos, those simple pleasures
we enjoy now, help me understand
that simplicity is a luxury beyond us.

Not Ready Yet

when i graduated i wish penn state's chancellor would've secretly written on my degree
the number of years i'd be enduring the vacant nods
of people not actually listening, believing, with their thirsty old plans tenured dry,

that i don't know anything i'm talking about—because i'll get carded for 12 more years,
& i'd wear bath towels out on Saturday nights if there were really no dress code,
& only now have i burst, a healthy hundred 45 from the cervix of my American education

into the wiry arms of the real world we exist separately from
until magically it's there, like a bookmark lost deep somewhere
in *Infinite Jest*,

materializing amidst our casual flipping of the pages, back & forth
for 23 years, 14 of which i barely remember—

so far flung for those 14 from any branch of credibility, why even live them?
if i know nothing now, then what have i been doing? me, some bull shit,

high off learning that's good, but not good enough to hold a gallon jug by itself,
weak with discreet artificiality like processed food,
not actually of this real world but a good imitation, a woman buried under make-up & dye,

pruned between tanning beds & summer after summer outside country concerts in the city,
drinking light beer on a plastic surgeon's pontoon—
wondering how else i can pretend to have what time
just isn't allowing me.

Texts with Friends, Part XI
To: Adrienne 9:46 PM, Saturday, 7/12/2014

You should've let me know.
I would've met you for booze.
We could've had dinner
and laid out on a blanket
in this clearing I sort of know
the way to, on Mt. Washington.

Just looked out over the city,
and the full moon tonight,
then got drunk, high, ate
way too many cheetos
and fell asleep.

It's a "super-moon," ya know?
According to the astrologists.

NEWS!

early one drunken morning,
in an eat n' park diner men's room,
a pittsburgh post-gazette enlightened me
on a new toilet that opens, closes itself

& bidets with such tenderness it's worth
the fifteen dehydrated sons & daughters
standing in puddles of their own feces
overseas putting it all together for us—

amazing where you can get news now—

& while i continue to relieve myself,
remembering the girls waiting back
at my table, sipping their milkshakes
& bobbing their heads to the tune

of another online pop sensation echoing
off these yellowed tiles; the pool of urine
around my own feet, tepidly reminds me
how advanced we are

In January, Crossing the Mississippi

from my Amtrak window seat,
a short story above the rails
i admire the water's arcane shifting,
thinking of Desoto, that resilient pusher onward,
piercing the skin of discovery's fruit,
building history along the banks
with the breath of the current's chest,
where so many arrived at their sweetest places,
these things i think, over the noise behind me—
the man from Baltimore   pushing,
spitting his game on Tiara, the girl sitting next to me,
& after three hours, finally getting
to jot her number into his phone—
"I might never see you again," he says,
"Sure you will. Just look me up," she answers.
the water is mostly frozen but we make our way
over a warm vein still pumping—he asks,
"Why don't we just go back in the lounge car
for a hot minute…?"   she shrugs "… Okay"
& they baby step into the dim gut
of our late-evening train,
"Oh shit! Shout out to the Mississippi!"
he yells, horny & grinning, leaving me—
looking dumbly out at the great American symbol
of conquest, the tradition continuing   the current
breathing quicker than ever

When I'm Depressed I Say Things Like

No one man ever accomplishes more than flossing the corn cob
from his teeth,
No one man ever accomplishes more than a good dump,
but when we laid together on the bathroom floor she said
her jumpsuit was like hummus,

No one man will ever perfect communication, or know the best way
to ignore the life insurance pitch of an old friend,
No one man will ever avoid those chance meetings
with awkwardness,
but when we laid together on the floor of sociology she said
her jumpsuit was like hummus,

No one man ever accomplishes more when he uses the words
wasteland, or ash, or eternity in a speech or poem,
No one man ever accomplishes Shakespeare's freshness of narrative,
but when we laid together on literature's floor she said
her jump suit was like hummus,

No one man will ever be able to discover without sounding
like an idiot to someone out there,
No one man will ever be able to prove that he completely
understands,
but when we laid together on the floor of knowledge she said,
her jump suit was like hummus,

No one man will stop those things we say we can stop by doing
the stuff we say will stop them,
No one man has a panacea for a thumb or any of his fingers,
but when we laid together on the floor of war she said
her jumpsuit was like hummus,

& when we laid there on the floor of staleness, exhaustion, boredom,
i looked over her, listing my inane conclusions, wanting her
to be serious with me, give me all the medicines
for being fooled by the grand schemes & she said
her jump suit was like hummus,
dip your knife, taste.

Eat 'n Park Poem

i came here with you,
to sit for 24 hours,
or however long we could stay
before we felt like we were
hurting our waitresses chances
at more, better tips

we listened to hits
of the '90s & conversations
about shitty work hours,
the hassle it must be
when people wait to be
seated & then tell the hostess
where they want to sit,

i look at you,
both of our plates filled
with salad bar, & i want you & i
to be that annoying couple,
in the booth over there
arms around each other
as our coffees get topped off
& cold again

topped off & cold again,
in the imaginary world
that we are really living in,
everything going our way,
regardless of where
the hostess seats us.

Texts with Friends, Part XV
To: Sadie 2:46 PM, Monday, 9/15/14

Paris will be fun.
And after that
i'll buy you
that big house
in the suburbs
you've always wanted.
With the white
picket fence and the monkeys
that pick exotic tea
from the canopies of our yard trees
and shit delicious coffee.
In the meantime, I'm hungry,
standing next to some weirdo
right now,
at subway.

Andy Feathers grew up in Pittsburgh, PA and remains alive today on a farm outside of Athens, GA. He earned his B.A. in Integrative Arts from Penn State University at Altoona, and co-directed Runaway Studios, a studio/arts show space with painter Sadie Shoaf from 2014-2015. In 2014, they co-founded "Runaway Hotel," a bi-annual art-book showcasing the visual and literary work of select emerging artists frequenting Runaway Studios and others around the U.S.

In addition to his poetry, script, and prose, he collaborates on visual art exhibitions under the name "The Three Little Pigs," enjoys street art, poster-making, and installation building when called upon. He seems to be unable to capitalize financially from any of these endeavors, so he also works as a beer vendor at PNC Park and Heinz Field, freelance journalist/proofreader, tutor, occasional contractor, baseball coach, and self-promoter.

He loves brewing—tea, coffee, beer, etc.—has a hound dog named Clown Shoes, and a pet pig named Almond Joy. Pigs live up to 25 years. He plans to stick to that commitment.

His work has been featured by *Festival Writer, Burningword Literary Journal, and The Copperfield Review,* among others, and he was nominated for a Pushcart Prize in 2014 by the Carbon Culture Review for his poem "Letters for a Lover in the Land before Texting." This is his first full collection.

www.ingramcontent.com/pod-product-compliance
Lightning Source LLC
Chambersburg PA
CBHW060225050426
42446CB00013B/3168